I Have Been to Minneota

★ ★ ★

RUDYARD THURBER

Copyright © 2014 by Rudyard Thurber

I Have Been to Minneota

All rights reserved. No part of this book may be reproduced in any form by any electronic or mechanical means including photocopying, recording, or information storage and retrieval without permission in writing from the author.

ISBN-13: 978-1-936449-64-4

Cover Design & Interior Layout: Ronda Taylor, www.taylorbydesign.com

Banyan Tree Press
Englewood, Colorado
Austin, Texas
www.banyantreepress.com

Printed in U.S.A

Contents

Acknowledgments vi
Dedication vii

Just So—So Stories

Cornerstones 1
Nineteen 7
Why I Was Pulling For the Mayans 9
Lesson Learned 11
Train Wreck 13
Goldie 15
Dad's Big Laugh 17
Mirror Image (For Roger and Chuck) *19*
The Problem of Justice 21
The Unholy Sacrifice of the Math 23
Forgery 25
Class Dismissed 27
Griddle Me This 29
Tongues 31
Trickle of Blood 33
Hometowns 35
Hobo at the Gate 37
Ends and Odds 39

NUANCES

Tumbleweed 43
Superannuation 44
Catch and Release 45
Roadbed 46
The Last Quiet Day 47
I Have Been to Minneota 48
The Girl Who Could See Around Corners 49
Lonely 50
Convalescence 51
Venn Diagram 52
Twenty Inches of Spring 53
Tabula Rasa 54
Party Time 55
Wake Me Before It's Over 56

NEEDS MUSIC

Phone It In 59
Starting Over 60
Curbside Pickup 61
Stowaway 62
Lock Me 63
About the Author 65
Interview of Tom Kinway (Transcribed from memory) . . . 66

Other Books by This Author

Rack and Wruin. Banyan Tree Press, 2011

Farmgirl. Banyan Tree Press, 2012

Acknowledgments

It's not been easy, as you might have guessed, to publish books of mixed format. I have been blessed to have found publishers who have been open to this variety, Dr. Patricia Ross and George Gluchowski at Banyan Tree Press. Thank you so much for your trust through three books now.

Many thanks, also, to my editor, Nancy Green, especially for the *pro bono* aspect of your work.

Finally, thanks to these who have read and given feedback on individual topics.

Rudyard Thurber

Dedication

This work is lovingly dedicated to the memories of Luke and Margaret Justyna and their beautiful grandmother, Dolores, who has been my bride and inspiration for many wonderful years.

I also dedicate this work to two true gentlemen that resolved their very different pains with a common solution. Herm and Wayne, it was truly a privilege to know you.

Just So—So Stories

Rudyard Thurber

Cornerstones

Do you think of Heaven as a place devoid of industry? Don't. A most important industry is conducted there. Babies are formed. In this place, there are several important stations. At one, toes and fingers are attached. At the Gendering station the child is so categorized. At the Metering station, they are pre-programmed with a discrete number of heartbeats, blinks for each eyelid, yawns and hiccups. At another, anomalies are inserted to pre-selected children. At yet another, Jesus Himself is working. Here He places a hand over the scalp of the baby. Several things happen. He numbers and maps all the hairs that will grow on this head. He also injects a spark of spirit to the child. He makes sure to touch every one.

At the last station, the umbilical cord is attached. The child is then presented to its mother.

Septapus

In a park near the lake in Collingwood there is this tree. It has seven trunks of similar diameter and height. Standing in the middle of them is like being a spectator of a cage match with seven fighters of comparable abilities.

Almost every day, a nondescript fellow of indeterminate age comes by to spend some contemplative time there. One day, a child showed up. It was Opal.

"Hi, there." offered Opal.

"Hey—how are you?" came the reply.

"What's your name? Mine's Opal."

"You can call me Merle," he said.

"Do you like this tree, too?"

"Yes," Said Merle. "I call it Septapus."

"Why do you call it that?" she asked with her head tilted.

With a smile he carefully explained the name.

She absorbed the information; then said, "My mom called this the tree of days."

"Very interesting. Why does she call it that, Opal?"

"She used to say when God was creating the universe that it was such a big job. He needed what she said were benchmarks. So, He made this special tree and at the end of each day of creating, He would add a trunk to the tree. After seven trunks, He knew He was done. I used to know which trunk went with which day, but I've forgotten."

"You have a wise mother, Opal."

"She's dead," she said simply.

Merle, of course, was taken aback by this bit of information.

"I'm sorry to hear that."

"It's okay. She's with God—something she always wanted."

Opal, it turned out, lived in a foster home and skipped a lot of school. She was part of a small cohort of similar fortune. As he got to gradually meet and know the individuals in the group he was surprised by the positive outlook they had. He had fully expected the opposite.

Opal's Cadre

Although a definite grouping, it was essentially leaderless. It was as if they all could read each other's minds and even know ahead of time what the other was going to do or say. What was clearly needed here was a mission.

Merle knew opportunity when he saw it. He became like a mentor to the group. He began by assigning each of them a trunk of the tree. While symbolic, it did show each was equal in the group. Once they each got used to whom had which trunk, they began leaving folded up notes in the bark. Privacy was always respected.

Merle decided they needed a name and he chose "Cornerstones." At this time he suggested the mission to look for opportunities to do good in their life.

These are the Cornerstones:

Charlesberg—Nobody ever did find out his first name.

Amelia—the quietest of the group. Of Jewish descent, her version of the seven trunks had to do with the seven sons in 2Maccabees.

Myron—He seemed to be the one most eager for the mission.

Esther—She was the only one with siblings yet at home.

Lloyd—Even at an early age he loved running.

Opal—the comedienne in the group. She had a knack for finding the absurd in almost everything.

Terry—Studious, open, often contentious.

All in all, Merle thought, a group with key overlaps of strength and a keen sense of fairness.

The Mission Years

It wasn't really a focus group but deciding on missions was a participatory event. The group soon found the real challenge was scoping the larger mission down into achievable tasks. There were a lot of inputs, a lot of needs identified. Merle carefully pointed out that the missions were life-long, so they should choose wisely as they were still youngsters.

Myron was especially anxious to start so Merle steered them to a project that could involve him.

Esther wanted a project involving a family. Terry offered to help whoever needed it.

Eventually they were all doing their missions either alone or with another Cornerstone.

Over time, as the kids grew up, some moved away. Some got married and had no more spare time, but the rest continued their missions faithfully.

Winning the Race

Lloyd, now thirty-four, decided to run the London Marathon. He had run marathons before and usually finished with a kick. Besides, he had always wanted to see London.

The day of the race started out cool. Perfect for running. As he ran, Lloyd had many thoughts about his life. He felt very blessed. He decided to bring back a small gift for each of the Cornerstones.

As he turned into the homestretch he was filled with happiness.

Then, he collapsed.

The marathon was marshaled with many fine medical people and he got attention immediately. It didn't matter. His meter had run out of ticks.

Upon hearing the news, Merle visited Septapus for the last time. He took a piece of paper out of one of his many pockets, read what it said, then folded it up and placed it in the bark of Lloyd's trunk.

Cornerstones was now over.

Merle began the slow trudge homeward. He knew it wouldn't be his last, but he would miss this bunch. They had worked hard and each *had* made a difference. He headed eastward on the County Line road. About a mile out of town it jogged right to get around a piece of forest on the left. Merle headed for the ditch and went into the forest. There was a trail here that only a practiced eye would find.

If you were still in town and watched Merle go home, you might have noticed a transformation occurring. He appeared to be getting shorter. His hat changed from a dusty old derby to a pointed, cone shaped one that looked hundreds of years old. Indeed, it was.

About a mile into the woods a house appeared. It looked English in construction. The smell of supper on the stove filled the air.

As Merle entered, he was greeted. "Welcome home, brother Merlin."

Merlin's brother, Cathcart, was standing over the kitchen stove where he was brewing venison stew.

"Wart called. He and Gwen are coming over later to play Whist."

"Okay" responded Merlin quietly. He was thinking he would be glad for the company.

Many years earlier he had arranged for Arthur and Gwen to escape their legacy, and they had lived quietly in the area ever since.

Merlin poured himself a cup of tea and announced, "I'm going to lie down for a few minutes, okay?"

Did You?

Did you figure out ahead of time who Merle was? Go back to the listing of the Cornerstones and see if a clue jumps out.

Rudyard Thurber

Nineteen

Nineteen gets no respect. Not that I am a numerologist, but what is (are) your recollections about nineteen? None, right? Okay—it's your nervous breakdown.

One is primary, of course. It has several appellations like "First" and "Primary." Even Unitarians think in terms of one. Two is almost as prevalent. There are still some holdouts (me included) that think when two become as one it's a man and a woman. Second is often likened to kissing your sister. Eyes and ears usually come in pairs. Three is a big number in the Bible. There are four gospels and four seasons (except here in Minnesota). And, four bases in baseball, softball, and weaveball. Five can be found populating our money system in its native value or its many multiples.

Six is the number of white horses come to carry me home. Seven is often linked with eleven in a dice game as well as the number of days commonly associated with creation and rest. Eight is for a crazy card game. By sheer coincidence it is also the number of sides in an octagon. There are nine days to a novena and, amazingly in another coincidence, there are nine balls used as targets in nine ball. Ten years is a decade and the number of little Indians in an Agatha Christie mystery. (Please don't call or write!)

Eleven was addressed in the paragraph above but is also the number of oceans. At least that's what the title *Ocean's Eleven* wants us to believe. Twelve has its own word—dozen—and is the number of original disciples of Jesus. Twelve is also the number of teams in the Big Ten. All those for throwing more money at higher education raise their right hand. Thirteen is sometimes called a baker's dozen and, in a conflict I will not resolve, there are actually thirteen oceans. Fourteen is the number of Stations of the Cross and, again, we have a unique term *fortnight* representing fourteen days and nights. Fifteen is an age common for driver permits and the number of men on a dead man's chest. What? Yo Ho Ho and a bottle of Perrier.

Sixteen is made famous in song and story. *Sixteen Candles*. Sweet sixteen and never been kissed. "I am sixteen going on seventeen." So on. Oh yeah—driver's *licenses*. When I was seventeen it was a very good year. Eighteen yellow roses came today. Nineteen. Hmmnn. Here we are.

This summer, my bride and I will celebrate nineteen years of marriage. I hope to give some meaning to the number nineteen.

Rudyard Thurber

Why I Was Pulling For the Mayans

This past December, humankind came face-to-face with its greatest conundrum. As Loretta Lynn (I think) put it "Everybody wants to go to Heaven but nobody wants to die."

The world was troubled by the Mayan calendar which seemed to end in December past.

What troubles me about all this is their reason for being troubled. I'm sure most people felt they weren't ready yet for the end of time as we know it. Apparently, they think they will be at some later date.

HELLO!

We're humans! We will never be ready! Now we only have more time to get more of our things caught in the wringer! When the time does finally come, we will need even more mercy.

Maybe it's my seniorness that sees the futility in waiting. But I certainly can understand why young people want more time. And, maybe—just maybe God is teasing or testing us with all the projected dates of destruction.

I wouldn't put it past Him.

Rudyard Thurber

Lesson Learned

About twenty-five years ago, I used to frequent an Episcopal church in a very old part of town. Most of the members, including the pastor, were Native Americans.

The signpost outside the church said services were at 10:30 and I was always at least a few minutes early. The old church had a gathering space apart from the worship space. Parishioners would always fill the gathering space and visit before the services.

Church service never started on time. Anywhere between 10:40 and 10:55 they would all rise together, unprompted, and enter the worship space. The side of me that needed and depended on structure was very confused.

Finally, one Sunday, as I'm sitting in the gathering space with others, I had to ask the question "Why do we never start on time?" A very polite lady then said to me, as if instructing a child, "We start Indian time."

Rudyard Thurber

Train Wreck

Intramural-level sports never makes the newspapers nor ESPN but can be just as entertaining.

Many years ago I played in a corporate league. The level of play was casual and many of the players worked daily with opponents and were, often, friends of long standing.

During one game, my own team had the bases loaded with no outs. Looked like a big inning shaping up.

The batter chopped a bouncer towards third base. The fielder there picked it clean and set his feet to throw home. The runner on third started towards home but, apparently, had second thoughts. He stopped about halfway there and turned back to third.

It's bad enough when one team is screwing up but this started an epidemic.

The third baseman saw the runner decommit towards home and double-clutched his throw but didn't let the ball go. At this point, instincts sort of set in and he decided to get the runner headed to first. This, of course, caught the first baseman a little off guard but he recovered nicely even though the runner beat the throw.

The first baseman, noticing a big crowd at third, felt this was the best place to get an out. He threw a return toss to the third baseman.

I need to tell you something about our runner on third. He was a bit of a rummy and, to be honest, may have been sampling before game time. Nevertheless, he was sober enough to see the runner who had emigrated from second and was now standing on third with a determination to not give it up.

Our runner who had been on third and who accurately assessed the look on the runner just described understood his only haven was home so he headed that way.

Of course, he made it. Final tally—one run, bases still loaded and no one out.

Our league played on Friday evenings and this was a perfect giggle for both sides to end the week.

I don't remember who won but I remember hearing a voice that sounded like Al Michaels muttering from the stands "Do you believe in miracles?"

Rudyard Thurber

Goldie

No two farm dogs are the same, yet they all have one thing in common. They all strive to become integrated family members.

Goldie was one of our farm dogs. She was a brown dog, easy to love and play with.

One day the family was on an outing. When we returned, this is what we found: A sow had escaped from the pen and Goldie had cornered her where the fence made a right turn.

Goldie had apparently taken a nip at the sow and drawn blood. By the time we got there, Goldie had eaten a good portion of the pig's left hip.

After the sow was rescued, Dad had to destroy Goldie. Our dad was created to farm and he loved both the soil and livestock. Putting the dog down must have been a terrible thing for our father. I'm sure, in his own quiet way, he loved Goldie as much as we kids did.

Over the years, farming must have brought a lot of heartache to our parents but they rarely showed it.

By the way, the sow survived.

Rudyard Thurber

Dad's Big Laugh

I ONLY REMEMBER MY DAD LAUGHING A COUPLE OF TIMES BUT, I cherish the memories.

He was of stoic stock, so laughing did not come naturally.

Often, after their retirement, my parents would go on bus trips with other seniors. One such trip landed them in Long Beach, at that time home of The Spruce Goose.

Dad sent me a picture of himself in the cockpit. Having worked for an airplane manufacturer in Seattle, I was impressed.

Some years later, I took my own family on a trip to California. I had to go see this magnificent wooden bird for myself. Imagine my surprise to find a mockup of the cockpit for photo taking.

When I next saw my dad, I confronted him with his trickery. Instead of contrition, I got hearty laughter. For years I thought he was laughing at me. It was only after reflecting that I now realized he was laughing at getting caught.

It was my dad being a kid again.

Rudyard Thurber

Mirror Image
(For Roger and Chuck)

I have this friend. Some years ago, she and her husband shucked their southern California climes for the chance to hunt and fish up in Missoula, Montana. Yes, they knew about winter.

I had this other friend. Some years ago, they left Missoula for southern California. Sometime, after several wonderful years in California, her husband was felled by a stroke with some follow-up TIAs.

Up in Montana, the husband recently had a stroke.

So what do we make of this? That God plays no favorites? That major moves late in life can be dangerous?

In both cases, the wives turned out to be real soldiers. Marines, even. They took over household management. In both cases this meant also overseeing modifications to the home that made life a little easier for the patients. Both ladies, selfless individuals before, became even more so after.

Here is what I glean from all this. Women are far tougher than men. Don't argue with me—I was in the delivery room for both my children.

This, of course, gets to the cleverness of women letting men think, all the time, that they were the tougher gender.

We men are such fools!

Rudyard Thurber

The Problem of Justice

For years I have been left with an empty feeling whenever the State exacts justice on a felon. Couldn't really define it until now.

Then, it came to me. Justice has very little, if anything, to do with survivors.

And, yet, it's the survivors who have to live with the consequences of the crime.

Take an extreme case of murder. In those few states still concerned with justice, the perpetrator might be given the death sentence. After the sentence is carried out, the authorities might congratulate themselves on achieving justice. But let us further suppose there is a surviving spouse and children. Where is their justice?

I'm sure this is not a new idea. If the felon had family of his or her own, this might seem to equalize. Execute someone close to the felon and make them watch. Then, give them an incarceration long enough for them to dwell on all this and, eventually, come to a point where they understand the impact of their deed. Who knows—this could lead to their salvation.

Of course, our very heritage and inherent sense of fair play would not allow this. But, it does serve to demonstrate the difficulty with justice.

Rudyard Thurber

The Unholy Sacrifice of the Math

I AM COMPLETELY UNQUALIFIED TO WRITE ABOUT THIS BECAUSE I am a man. There are those who would try to make me believe this. I choose not to.

I cannot look at any child and not think about this.

When you ask people how many participants it takes to get pregnant, most would answer "two." I think this number is a little short. When you look at a child, you should be struck by the uniqueness of each. This is elaborate engineering—something not earthly. In my mind, God has put His stamp of approval on this conception.

When, later, a couple or just the mother-to-be, decides to abort the baby, there is more than just a decision about the child going on here. There is an implicit decision to overrule the Lord.

This, it would seem to me, becomes the real sticky wicket on Pearly-Gate day. Not only will they have to try to explain their decision to take the life of an infant (for some this would be multiples), they will have to try to explain why they set themselves up above God in making this decision. False gods are rumored to make our God very angry.

I wonder how many people in this situation (including participating doctors) take the time to learn the real story of Norma McCorvey.

Rudyard Thurber

Forgery

It used to be that schooling was multi-faceted and didn't involve busing.

One of the facets, of course, was the home. It was there I learned the number of days in the month.

Thirty days have November
April, June, and September
All the rest have thirty one
Except February...

Included implicitly in the phrase "All the rest" is August. This becomes important to the story.

A trick the mind plays on you sometimes is, if you know something, you assume someone else might.

One year, when it became time to register kids for the St. Paul Parks and Recreation hockey program, I took my son to the orientation/signup meeting. During the signup, we were filling out a form when we came to the part about birthdays. The form stated that if the kid was born on or after September first he would be in one age group. Otherwise, if he was born on August thirtieth or before, he would be in another. Please don't get picky here. It's been over twenty years and I am loosely paraphrasing.

In any event, my son has a birthday that is August 31. No man's land. How someone with no credible grasp of calendaring was able to get his or her form okayed just befuddled me.

There were several avenues of remediation available. I could point out the mistake to the person in charge of our particular geography and just get an assignment for my son either way. I didn't really think this would happen.

I could take the issue downtown the next morning and hope for similar results. That seemed even less likely when there was an entire bureaucracy to protect.

I could try to talk my son out of hockey but any substitute probably used the same form.

It seemed simplest to use a fourth approach. Make the paperwork match the crime.

I asked my son which group of kids he wanted to play with since he knew all of them. He gave me an answer and, so, with the help of a copy of his birth certificate, an old portable typewriter, some whiteout, and a copy machine he now has an alternate birthdate.

I mean—it's not like he was Wayne Gretzky.

Rudyard Thurber

CLASS DISMISSED

I SUPPOSE THE REALIZATION FIRST CRYSTALLIZED UNDER REAGAN. I, of course, had felt moments of being uncomfortable with other politicians but this time it was an overt act of aggression towards fellow human beings. You may remember it differently than I do.

Instead of negotiating with air traffic controllers in good faith (or any kind of faith), he (Reagan) summarily cashiered the whole of our air-traffic controller fleet. Conveniently forgetting he, himself, was once active in a bargaining unit, he turned into the essence of republicanism.

This effort to eliminate the middle class has found great support under Obama.

Using not-so-clever smokescreens such as a Republican war on women they move to pick all the pockets of those still with a job.

At the rate they are going they are clearly splitting the country into haves and have nots. What is truly fascinating about all this is how so many current haves have been sucked into the maelstrom. It will be really interesting when he moves in with the liberal *coup de grace* and tries to divvy up what's left of this country's wealth. Talk about a dumb idea. One clue that this is a dumb idea will be that Hollywood supports it.

If one thinks to ask "How can Democrats do this?" it's because they themselves have become rich at the public trough. They are now in league with Republicans.

Nevertheless, except for the fact you will never get full value for any of them, politicians are a bargain. I mean, think about this the next time you vote: You get two assholes for the price of one.

Rudyard Thurber

Griddle Me This

Home ownership is not for the chickenhearted.

In our first house was a monster stove. It had four burners and a hotplate in the middle. One day, I decided to try it out by frying an egg on the griddle.

I cracked the egg and put the contents in the center of the griddle. I turned around to do something and, when I turned back, the egg was gone.

"Where did my damn egg go?" I shouted to no one in particular although my wife happened to be standing nearby. For some unexplained reason, she decided sympathy was not required but laughter was. And, laugh she did to my rising anger. I couldn't decide who to be angry at—her or the stove that ate my egg.

It turned out that the stove wasn't level. Have you ever tried to clean a stove with burnt egg in its internal workings?

What about the family we bought the house from? How long had they lived with an un-level stove? They were building a house and did the husband, acting as a general contractor, ever use a square or level in its construction?

There were other lessons with our first house. One is: Never buy a house on a steep hillside. You will eventually have to mow it.

Rudyard Thurber

Tongues

My bride and I frequently play cards at various senior centers. At one center, there was a very nice gentleman (now deceased) who was a delight to play with. He always had a twinkle going despite his ninety-some years.

One day, at a table where I was partnered with him, it was his turn to bid. The game we played was called Five Hundred. In this game, players get only one bid, and usually the first bidder in a partnership would do what we call "Inkle" with a six bid to indicate a jack or joker.

He tried to bid inkle but the word came out as a foreign language. The gentleman tried again but no change. He was becoming frustrated and, after several tries, just showed the joker. We all were curious although I was concerned he might be having a stroke. No-one understood what he was saying. Another senior, Gerheart by name, tried to talk to him in German.

Nothing.

The EMTs came and checked him out but found nothing amiss.

Next week we were all abuzz when Ollie showed up, twinkle and all, speaking perfect English. As a group, we assumed he had grown up in a multilingual household but, it turns out, he had never spoken anything other than English. Go figure.

Rudyard Thurber

Trickle of Blood

I am soon to be sixty eight years old. How I got to this number involves a succession of miracles.

At an intersection of township roads just east of our farmstead one of the ditch corners was filled with willow trees. This provided an eye obstruction for cars coming from the East or South.

The County hired me to cut down the willow saplings. One of the commissioners even had a tool for me to use. It was a machete.

This machete was about a six inches by fifteen inches plate of steel. At the far end from the handle, on the top of the blade, the machete had a curl of sharp steel ending in a point. Also, the handle had a steel loop for the active hand to use as a pivot. You could really build up speed with this feature.

One afternoon, after school, I was hacking away when my ear felt wet. I remember thinking "That's odd. I've never had my ears sweat before." I went to wipe away the sweat and found blood instead. After some probing, I found a cut in my scalp left there by the point of the curl as I was pivoting along. Just a slight effort one way or another, and I would have punctured my skull.

Alone in that ditch, it would have been too late by the time someone from my family found me.

I eventually finished the job, but I did it without the machete.

Rudyard Thurber

Hometowns

"Rust grows along the railroad track
The young folks leave and they don't comeback."
"Our Little Town"
Greg Brown, Iowan poet

IF YOU ARE OF RURAL HERITAGE YOU MIGHT BE A LITTLE CONFUSED about your hometown. For example, I have always thought of the town where I went to school as my hometown. Yet, that is pretty much all I ever did there. However, there is so much more to the formation of an adult.

I matriculated all those years in a town called Iroquois. Was in the same school building for twelve years. Haven't been back. Iroquois, true to its Scandinavian roots, was home to a character named Cowboy Ole.

A town closer to our farm was Esmond, a ghost town once saluted on *Hee Haw*. *Hee Haw* salutes Esmond, South Dakota—population four! (All together) SALUTE!"

It still has two enterprises as far as I know—a Methodist church where I was once baptized and a cemetery.

When the railroad was viable, Esmond did pretty well. People would come up from Carthage or down from Iroquois. Esmond was on a railroad diagonal between these two towns. And, people still rode the trains.

We did our grocery shopping in Esmond. There were two grocery stores to choose from: Hemming and Vi Johnson's or Lila Wiles'.

Hemming had a mean streak. He welded a nickel to the floor and every time we tagged along we'd practically work our fingers bloody trying to get that damn nickel off the floor.

Every night around ten, Hemming would turn off the town's only streetlight.

I believe I've mentioned Carthage. A nice town my bride sometimes mispronounces as Cartridge. What you need to know about Carthage is this: Its water tower once caught on fire.

Carthage is where we did the most church stuff. Funerals especially. Many relatives had their services there.

I have many fond memories of Carthage including their quaint ballpark back in the days of town ball.

I also remember a coach from there offering to send their school bus to our farm if my brother and I would go to school there instead of Iroquois.

As I write this I begin to see how lucky I was for all these hometowns. In my other book, *Farm Girl*, I think I talked about Huron where I had many friends.

All of these work together to form the mosaic of me.

Rudyard Thurber

Hobo at the Gate

"**M**om! Someone is coming down the road!"
 We seldom had visitors way out in the country and this one was on foot. The person was far enough away we couldn't pick up any details yet.

After about fifteen more minutes, we could make out the visage of a man who looked to be about forty years of age. Hard times being what they are, he may have been 0nly thirty.

"It's a guy, Mom."

Our mother, a very intelligent woman, refused to learn how to drive, then complained that she never got to go anywhere. It was very annoying. Thus, she became quite animated at the prospect of meeting someone new.

When the itinerant traveler reached our long driveway, he hesitated only briefly, then turned towards our home.

Jesse, the oldest of us boys, often acted as interpreter of events. Naturally, we deferred to his wisdom. After all, Jesse was practically a teenager. Jolie, our only sister, was more the independent thinker and often challenged his readings. This probably had its payoff when Jolie became a captain in the women's Marine Corps.

While the man was walking towards our house, Jesse was giving commentary on the way the man was dressed.

"He's wearing a suit and tie. That must be hot walking."

Actually, unbeknownst to Jesse, he was talking about a cultural phenomenon that lasted until the late 1950s. Men wore suits. They would come home from work wearing a suit and change into a different one for supper. No matter the economic circumstances, a suit was in style.

This particular suited traveler was named Leland and he hailed from South Haven, Kansas where he had last worked at a filling station until the enterprise had been forced to close.

For some unexplained reason, Leland headed North instead of West. Perhaps for a factory job, perhaps to do something different from almost everyone else. He said he heard of hiring in Ramona but was going the opposite direction.

He had asked for a sandwich but Mom wouldn't hear of it and threw some precious corncobs into the stove. While leftovers were heating up, the man mentioned a wife and three sons back in Kansas.

When the man's lunch was ready, Mom sent us kids outside.

Later, as he was leaving, he had a bag which, I suppose, contained a sandwich or two. But, something seemed akilter with the picture. I couldn't quite put my finger on it, though.

That night over supper, we were telling Dad about the visitor. It was when Jesse started talking about the suit the man wore that it hit me. He had left without his necktie!

Rudyard Thurber

Ends and Odds

I may be old-fashioned but old fashioned has got me this far.

★ ★ ★

This may interest only older people: In a perfect world, there would be open season on packaging engineers.

★ ★ ★

Not that I am old but, when I got my first driver's license, I had to parallel park a horse and buggy.

★ ★ ★

I try to write with a wink.

★ ★ ★

Everyone seems worried about and planning for a meteorite or asteroid hitting the Earth. It seems to me we should also be concerned about something knocking the sun off its course.

★ ★ ★

At least once, when I was younger, I would have loved getting frisky with Mrs. Cunningham.

★ ★ ★

There can be no "Rap" in Heaven. Otherwise, it wouldn't be Heaven.

★ ★ ★

So many forks in the road of life. I might have become a country singer, but I had hay fever.

★ ★ ★

Miracles do happen. But we have to let them.

★ ★ ★

Marriage is a fifty-fifty deal. In ours, for example, she gets the credit, and I get the blame.

★ ★ ★

The reason we fear death is that we don't trust.

★ ★ ★

You can't beat the entertainment value of a baby.

★ ★ ★

"But, Hillary," Bill was trying to explain, "Monica didn't inhale either!"

★ ★ ★

There are no vegetarian cougars. They are all carnalvores.

★ ★ ★

Am I the only person who wishes Dairy Queen delivered?

★ ★ ★

Nuances

Rudyard Thurber

Tumbleweed

Coming out of nowhere
In a prairie ambush
The principle of whimsy
Rolling where it will.

The perfect wheel invented
And patented by God.
It teases as it rolls
"Follow me if you can."

I have a friend
Who calls herself this name
The word suggests action.
Movement. Adventure.

I wonder what it's like
To be so fancy free
Always with the past behind
Spinning
Spinning
Spinning always
into the not yet known.

SUPERANNUATION

Sometimes it feels to me
That I have always been this old.
The past keeps repeating
I am on my nth childhood.

My body is a mass of hurt.
My mind loses track.
Many friends are gone.
The seasons keep coming round.

Do I still need to be here?
Have I fulfilled my purpose?
Why do I need to see doctors
If I feel this way?

I see others fighting on
And wonder "Do I look like them?"
Good Grief—My kids are getting old
Did you think I wouldn't notice?

Rudyard Thurber

Catch and Release

Why do you do this?
Where is the joy?
Every time I see you
You have a new boy.

What's with all this sampling?
One after another.
Are none good enough
To be your true lover?

Are you looking for something
That just isn't there?
Having trouble deciding?
Have you forgot how to care?

Is there a challenge
To have some on the side?
In case something happens
Have you nothing to hide?

Roadbed

Troubadour, oh troubadour
Where will you spend the night?
The songs are done. The crowd has left.
They're turning out the light.

Your car's a running miracle.
Stay in the warmer clime.
Don't book a show that's too far north
And always, always rhyme.

The back seat holds your pillow.
A parking lot will do.
A good night's sleep, then stretch your legs.
Then, onto the rendezvous.

Rudyard Thurber

THE LAST QUIET DAY

The school is closed and shuttered
Like an abandoned factory
Which, I suppose,
Is what it is.

Tomorrow it will re-open
But, gone from Mrs. Kennedy's First Grade room
Will be Alyssa and Daniel
So the noise will be different.

Meet Tara and Ian
Who will pick up the baton
Without missing a beat
And the song goes on.

Mr. Talmidge, in Third Grade,
Had a breakdown over the summer.
No one knows
But Nick and Colby will quickly find his fragility

Noise takes many forms in a school
From openly aural to subtle acts.
These days, bullying is a form of noise.
Why are we so mean?

We keep promoting the noise
So they become someone else's problem.
There must be a statistical reason
All children are not meant to be model citizens.

I Have Been to Minneota

It was Nineteen Sixty Five
On my way back to South Dakota
I saw a sign "Minneota x mi. ➔"
A friend was teaching there
So, I turned North

It was a nice reunion
Filled with lots of catching up.
At this time
Neither of us
Had heard of Bill Holm

I'm not the sort of person
Who does pilgrimages
(Although, I have twice been to Lake Wobegon)
I have yet to meet Mr. Keillor there.
Perhaps he's just a myth.

Rudyard Thurber

The Girl Who Could See Around Corners

She said she came from France.
But I tried to not let
That get in the way.
She had a way
Of seeing the future
But had no desire to change it.
This bothered me some at first.
Especially when she knew
That I would leave
Before I knew.

Is prescience a feminine trait?
I, a Taurus,
Always charge ahead.
Never mind possible outcomes.

She said she came from France.
But, I tried to not let
That get in the way.

Lonely

I look out my window
And I see you
Walking on the macadam path
Alone.

I see you almost every day.
I look for you
And I wonder;
Are you lonely, too?

It seems to me such people
Almost always take the same path
As if they were looking for something
They might have lost.

But, I know
They aren't even paying attention
To where they are going.
Where *are* they going?

Rudyard Thurber

Convalescence

I suppose I will eventually heal
Of writing
In this life or the next.

I hope to get the blessing
Of Writers' Block
Instead of mismatched text.

It's all my readers' fault,
Of course,
That I am in this mess.

It once was fun but
Now is toil.
I just don't need the stress.

I've Been to Minneota

Venn Diagram

I hover around the edges
Of other people's lives
No longer the center
Of a circle of my own.

Each morning I look into the mirror
Not seeing the empty human
Going through the remaining motions
In the Winter of his life.

Over time, the circles grow bigger
As my presence in them shrinks
Until, one day, it dawns on me
I am no longer needed.

Rudyard Thurber

Twenty Inches of Spring

The calendar says "Play ball!"
The weather guy says "NO!"
"We have a blizzard moving in
And the wind is going to blow."

There's an old politician
A guy who's really fat
Who claims that global warming
Is really where we're at

I never trust a fat guy
Nor politician yet
Even if they claim
To have made the internet

Tabula Rasa

The mind is like a hideaway
Where lives both fear and hope
And things I think but do not write
Like "Why do men choose rope?"

It's a cave with many tunnels
Of ill-supported walls
With just a little jarring
A mental construct falls

If I could be a painter
The colors I would do
Would be, you see, primarily
The many shades of blue

It's not a pleasant place to go
So do not linger long
And know that it is difficult
To sort out right from wrong.

Rudyard Thurber

Party Time

The democrats are coming
To take our guns and knives
They think that they have been ordained
To completely run our lives

The republicans are running
Far, far away
We have no more money
So, why would they stay?

Tea Party folks are rigid
No compromise is found.
It's their way or no way
No such thing as common ground.

Independents have no stature,
No muscle on the floor.
It all sounds good in theory
But won't buy candy at the store.

I've Been to Minneota

Wake Me Before It's Over

I do not know when I will die
But, die I know I shall
Right now I do not feel afraid
To wear the dead one's pall

But, this is not about my death
Or what measures you might take
It's time to celebrate for me
It's time to plan my wake!

Bring the parson in for prayers
And family to shake hands
Add those who'll say how nice I look
Have flowers in their stands

Set up tables all around
In case some cards break out
Acoustic music would be nice
So you can twist and shout

I can't stand organ music
So unplug the thing for now
Find someone to tell some tales
No "holier than thou."

Needs Music

Rudyard Thurber

Phone It In

We will probably never meet
Yet, we are old friends.
I keep your voice on speed dial
For those times that lonesome sends.

You have a laugh I cherish
And a spirit I can feel
At times I long to come to you
To see if you are real.

In truth, you have become my distant muse
You set me right when thinking goes astray
When worries mount and all seems lost there's you
As endless night turns into endless day

May you always be there
When I get lost amid the verse
To steer me and to laugh with me
My literary nurse.

In truth, you have become my distant muse
You set me right when thinking goes astray
When worries mount and all seems lost there's you
As endless night turns into endless day

Starting Over

Let's pretend tonight that we are single
And have caught each other's eye
I'll ask you to dance a dance with me
And you'll do so acting shy

We move across the wooden floor
Lost in our encoupled space
I am wholly captivated by
Your sweetness and your grace

Of course I'll fall in love again
And, when the dance is through
Will not want to let you go
I will know that it is you

I breathe you in and hold you tight
I sense a memory there
From years ago when we were young
And love's enticements filled the air

Of course I'll fall in love again
And, when the dance is through
Will not want to let you go
I will know that it is you

Rudyard Thurber

Curbside Pickup

I see you standing at the corner
Waiting for the bus.
If I don't stop to talk to you
There'll never be an "us."

I pull up to the sidewalk
And roll the window down.
As if old friends I offer you
A ride on into town.

As if old friends you jump right in
Grateful for the ride
I'm stumped for things to talk about
With you so close beside.

I ask "Where can I take you?"
Then, quiet fills the van.
"Wherever it is you're going."
"I like a generous man."

We roll into the city.
I find a likely spot.
I say, "Is this okay?"
Hoping that it's not.

Stowaway

You climbed into my heart
When I was away.
Hiding there amongst my issues
'Til I found you one lost day.

You asked if it would be okay
To hide out for a spell
Within the channels of my heart.
You made me promise not to tell.

So now you are my secret
One I carry all the while.
Not sure what to do with you
Lately, all I do is smile.

Rudyard Thurber

Lock Me

Lock me down. Take away my keys.
I won't be going anywhere without these.

Lock me down. Sell my old car.
Without it I won't get too far.

Lock me down. Hide all my pants.
Don't give me a second chance.

The honky-tonk is calling
I can hear its plea
Will you go in my place
And have a drink for me?

Lock me up, oh constable
I'm hiding from my wife.
If I get caught the sentence is
Nothing less than life.

The honky-tonk is calling
I can hear its plea
Will you go in my place
And have a drink for me?

Lock me up, oh constable
I'm hiding from my wife.
If I get caught the sentence is
Nothing less than life

About the Author

Rudyard Thurber is not my real name. If I look up and see no drones or someone recording what is going on, I use the name of Jim Johnson. My mother, in a spiritual moment, gave me the middle name of "Wesley" in hopes I would become a Methodist preacher.

I later became Catholic.

I have absolutely no trust in government. One of our sons, a conspiritoralist claims there is only one party—the incumbents.

One day I was walking near a lake when I heard screams for help. I looked out and saw someone thrashing about on the far side of the lake. I looked down and found a rope at my feet. I bent down and picked it up. I was just about to throw it when I recognized the drowning person. It was a politician. I dropped the rope and went to the waters edge. I began to spit in their direction, you understand, to expedite the drowning process. I, too, try to be a good citizen.

Just then a kayaker floated near the non-swimmer. It was a lobbyist. He threw two bags of money at the politician. They acted as flotation devices. The politician kicked to shore.

Foiled yet again.

As with my last book *Farmgirl*, I hope this is my last one. However, in case I find more to write about, I continue to interview for help. One such interview is recorded here.

I Have Been to Minneota

Interview of Tom Kinway
(Transcribed from memory)

RUDYARD THUBER: "Welcome, Mr. Kinway."

TOM KINWAY: "My pleasure, Mr. Thurber."

RUDYARD THURBER: "I am looking for someone with writing experience to help me if I write another book. Did you ever write a book?"

TOM KINWAY: "No, but I did ride a horse."

RUDYARD THURBER: "I'm not sure that applies here… "

TOM KINWAY: "I was on a water polo team."

RUDYARD THURBER: "Could we please get back to my agendum?"

TOM KINWAY: "I found out later that my horse didn't know how to swim."

RUDYARD THURBER: "I'm sorry to hear that. Perhaps he could take lessons."

TOM KINWAY: "He drowned."

RUDYARD THURBER: "I'm so sorry to hear that. Have you ever thought of writing about this experience?"

TOM KINWAY: "Did you know horses poop when they die?"

RUDYARD THURBER: "No, I didn't know that."

TOM KINWAY: "I looked around and there was just me and the poop and Carlyle in the pool."

RUDYARD THURBER: "Your horse was named 'Carlyle?'"

TOM KINWAY: "It was secretly 'Lightning' but, it was a rule that the horses had to have an Ivy League name to be in the conference.

RUDYARD THURBER (Giving up): "So, what happened?"

TOM KINWAY: "Well, eventually, the poop broke up into smaller pieces but the bottom of the pool was really a mess."

RUDYARD THURBER: "No! What happened to the horse - to Carlyle?"

TOM KINWAY: "I guess he's still there, all 1300 pounds of him."

RUDYARD THURBER: "Thank you for your time, Mr. Kinway."

www.ingramcontent.com/pod-product-compliance
Lightning Source LLC
Chambersburg PA
CBHW022108040426
42451CB00007B/186